The Art Of Letting Go

The Art Of Letting Go

THOUGHT CATALOG

Thought Catalog Books

Brooklyn, NY

Contents

1

Rania Naim

Letting go is really hard, especially when you have to let go of something you really want, whether it's an opportunity, or someone you really liked or loved, or even any expectations you had about something. I don't think anyone knows how to completely let go or not fall back from time to time if they do, but there are definitely ways to make it easier for you to let go when you relentlessly don't want to let go.

1.

What is destined will reach you, even if it be
underneath two mountains. What is not destined,
will not reach you, even if it be between your two lips.
—Proverb

Anything that feels forced or harder than it should be or causes you pain and distress is not meant for you. Having this mentality or faith will help you overcome the reluctance that comes with making a decision of whether or not you should let go. Things that are meant for you have a way of flowing smoothly into your life. The more you fight for something that is not meant for you, the more it will fight you. You may get what you want in the end, but it may not last and you may not feel at ease with it. The beauty of things that are meant for you is that they just happen; against all odds. We are just programmed to complicate life sometimes.

2.

The only thing more unthinkable than leaving was staying; the only thing more impossible than staying was leaving.
—Elizabeth Gilbert

Letting go is really painful when you feel "stuck," and it can sometimes seem impossible to do, but the truth is if you reach this point, it means that you've been trying so hard to make this thing work in your favor, or reach your goal, and it sometimes feel like we've tried so hard or come a long way that if we let go now, it will feel like a waste of time given the time and effort we invested in it. But nothing is a waste of time, even if it feels like it, we are here to make mistakes and learn lessons to grow as individuals, if we keep holding on to toxic situations or toxic people because we've already done too much or it's too late to change things, we are only setting ourselves up for a miserable life. There is power in letting go, a power that brings more peace and serenity than being stuck in situations that make your heart a bit heavier each and every day.

3.

*If you're brave enough to say goodbye, life will reward
you with a new hello.*
—Paulo Coelho

This outlook really helps you move on and let go faster. Same
notion that when one door closes another opens. Life opens
new doors for you all the time; imagine you are a key to
multiple doors and you just think you can only open one
door. We have so much potential, so many talents, so many
kind things to give back to the world. We have so many keys
to open so many doors. When you leave one door behind
and lock that door, you will be surprised by the number of
doors that were waiting to be open by you and only you. Some
endings are not bad; sometimes they are not even endings,
just bridges to new beginnings.

4.

*I think part of the reason we hold on to something so
tight is because we fear something so great won't
happen twice.*
—Anonymous

Here's another reason why we hold on to things or people
longer than we should. We convince ourselves that good
things won't happen twice; we will not be able to find someone
who is that great again or who makes us feel this way again.
Or we won't be able to find a job like that again, or something

we are that passionate about again. The truth is, you will always find something or someone that makes you feel this way again, new passions will emerge and good things will happen twice and as many times as they want, and will probably be a better and more convenient fit for you. If you look back at your life, you will find yourself laughing at certain situations when you thought you would never move on, or how you held on to something so tightly. Great things happen to us all the time in different shapes or forms; we just like to focus on the things that are not so great. Holding on to something out of fear that it will never happen again, is the definition of fear. We have to be fearless in letting go.

5.

See it for what is, not what you want it to be.
—Anonymous

The truth is if you reach a point where letting go is the only option, it usually means that this thing or someone already let you go. You are trying to stay in a place where you are not welcome anymore. The mind has a funny of way of tricking us into believing certain things to make it less painful for us, or put it in a way that doesn't really hurt our pride or break our heart, but we have to look at it the way it is, the way it is being portrayed to us, not the way we want to see it. This is not an optical illusion, this is reality, and in reality, what you see is what you get. If an opportunity passed you by, it didn't really want to stop at your station, if someone let you go, they didn't really want to stay, if someone else got what you were praying for, this blessing was not written for you to begin with and you will be blessed in another way. As you keep learning the art of letting go, let go of your fear, of your past, of your mistakes, of your insecurities, of your failures, of your self-doubt. Forgive yourself enough to let go of even the parts of you that dim your light.

2

13 Things To Remember When You Realize He's Not Right For You

Skyla Child

I've always believed that it's easier to be hurt, than it is to hurt someone else. I have told myself so many times – he's the right guy for someone, just not the right guy for me. As long as I can remember, I thought that being in a relationship for a few years means you are destined to be lifelong partners. It's only recently that I discovered this isn't true. I know that I can't be the only one in this situation, so for those who need it – cheers to the following lessons learned.

1. I've learned that no matter how long you've been together – when you know, you know. It's entirely possible to be with someone for five years, yet still not be right for each other permanently.

2. You don't meet people by accident, and that each person who crosses your path brings life lessons to you that God knew you needed. Everyone you meet makes you stronger, and makes you look at life just a little different than you did before.

3. Count on your family. For years I've considered my significant other my constant, which is true to an extent…but, I've learned that your true constant throughout life is the family that God blessed you with. Never forget who you are, and where you come from.

4. Don't lose who you are, even if you don't know yourself yet. In life, we are constantly reinventing ourselves, but don't give up things you once loved and sacrifice your independence.

5. It's hard to let go, but it's harder to be unhappy. Some happiness is only temporary and sometimes making a hard decision requires you to find happiness that isn't.

6. A relationship should bring out the best in you. A relationship should be eternally supportive, and you should lift each other up in your worst moments.

7. Mistakes help us find the right person in the long run. Mistakes help you grow, and be better for the next person that you share your heart with.

8. Read quotes, and listen to LOTS of music. I can't tell you how many times reading endless quotes on the internet lifted my spirits and gave me clarity. Music has been my savior through so many challenging times.

9. You have to truly love yourself, inside and out, before you can be in a successful relationship. We learn to love ourselves more and more each day through growth. Making our own independent decisions without seeing them through someone else's eyes, helps us to find out who we truly are.

10. Life. Gets. Better. Sometimes it's hard to see past tomorrow or next week. It's easy to get caught up in this moment, and think about how bad it is without realizing that with time, things will start to look up for you again.

11. Open your eyes to every opportunity. You never know what could change your life next. Sometimes being in a relationship can fog your choices, but it's important to take opportunities that will help you grow.

12. Be brave, and be bold. I learned that no matter how hard it is, it's so important to say what you mean, and mean what you say. Not only are you being honest with others, but being honest with yourself.

13. Follow your heart, and your brain alike. One isn't more important than the other, they both matter equally. It's important to make smart decisions, that back up your emotional feelings.

3

I'm Glad It Didn't Work Out Between Us

Marisa Bagnato

I'm glad it didn't work out between us.

Well, all of you. (And by 'you' I mean my exes.) But nobody in specific.

Thank you for not only falling short of my expectations, but for giving me new reasons to have higher ones. Thank you for personifying every person's nightmare in a relationship: For the cheating, lying, emotional abuse, and indifference. Thank you for giving me those experiences, only because they allowed me to determine what my lines were, and when you crossed them. I am indebted to your actions – they made my skin so thick, that you can't even see the blood course through my veins anymore. Yet, I am still alive.

I'm not trying to say you were all bad. Truthfully, you had good aspects – that's why we dated, ex-boyfriends. But they were not enough to keep us together. They could not satiate me and my need to be respected, appreciated, or valued. And the sole reason for that is simple: I respect, appreciate, and value myself far too much to have stayed. Thank you for letting me go, thank you for letting me leave.

Your indifference taught me that I could not be indifferent to my own needs, ex-boyfriends. And that is a powerful lesson that I might not have learned had you not been so dismissive of me. Your emotional abuse and manipulative tactics taught me I could not tolerate being disrespected. I give respect, and I deserve it back – from everyone.

Your lies and deceit made me realize how much I valued myself, my body, and the right to leave a situation that puts either in danger.

I did not need you to learn these things, ex-boyfriends. But thanks to you, I learned it sooner. My experience has helped me see how much power there is in being alone. I took some time to reflect on my choices. I realized that, too often, I spent time on people who didn't think of me half as much. I gave to people who could only take. I loved people who could only give me apathy. I grew from this.

I had an epiphany in that time: That those things you did to me bothered me, hurt me, and destroyed me, and they did so because deep down, I knew I deserved better. I wanted better. And in order to find that, I had to treat myself with dignity, respect, and love. A lot of love.

I'm not trying to hurt you, ex-boyfriends. I also don't have any real hard feelings. I'm in a good place, a place I never would've reached with you. And if that truth is a devastating one, I am sorry. But I am not sorry for needing, deserving, and wanting more for myself.

I hope you change the things that take people away from you, and that you find happiness – alone or with another person. I hope you grow from the things you did, too.

But really, I'm so thankful it didn't work out between us.

It worked out just great for me.

4

6 Ways To Move On After Heartbreak That Will Begin To Heal The Pain

Sabrina Alexis

When I was 17, I experienced an important rite of passage...my very first heartbreak. And it was more brutal and agonizing than anything I could ever have imagined. He was a boy I met at a party who stirred me in a way I can't quite articulate.

I felt something that no one else had ever made me feel before, and no one has since.

We talked every day, hung out on weekends, and he had this way of just making me feel alive, of making me feel like everything was OK. It ended because I wanted things to be more serious and he was a freshman in college and wanted to be young, stupid, and free, not tied to a relationship.

I was absolutely devastated, crushed, gutted from the inside out.

I was interning at *US Weekly* magazine at the time and what I most remember from that period was replaying everything about our relationship on loop every morning as I took the train into the city, and every evening on my way back home. I couldn't stop, no matter how much it hurt.

I didn't properly deal with the pain and it followed me like a piece of toilet paper stuck to the bottom of a shoe. I always had a feeling of not being good enough, a fear that the guy wouldn't want me the way I wanted him.

My next major heartbreak came a few years later when I was 21. This time was even worse because the relationship was a lot more serious, and a lot more toxic. The end was also much more devastating. He left me for someone else, and once again I didn't process it properly; instead, I let it fester and eat away at me and I developed an even stronger complex about not being good enough, about not being worthy of getting the love I truly wanted.

These breakups both caused an insurmountable amount of pain but also brought a lot of good.

The end result? I ended up marrying the high-school ex, and I started this website with the college ex and get to write about relationships for a living. So I guess it's true that all's well that ends well!

But back to the matter at hand: How to get over a breakup. They say time heals, and in some ways this is true, but it takes more than time. You also have to process the situation, you need to digest, you need to feel, you need to make peace, you need to get in touch with your inner strength, and you need to move on as a better, stronger person than you were before. This is not how I handled either of those breakups.

What I did was obsess and replay everything that happened and what I wish I had done differently. Then I got lost in an endless array of distractions. I was going, going going, keeping myself busy so I wouldn't have to feel anything. I took it all way too personally and these feelings of inadequacy bled into almost every relationship I had after.

Here is something to keep in mind about pain: it doesn't go away just because it goes unacknowledged. The more you avoid it, the more it merges into your psyche and becomes a part of you. These faulty beliefs get wired in and will remain unless you challenge them.

But let's get a little more concrete and talk about how to get over a breakup the right way.

1.Don't Take it Personally

I know it feels personal, I know it feels like you weren't good enough, that you should have done something else, been some other way. But it's not. Sometimes the timing just isn't right (as was the case with my high-school ex/current husband), or sometimes two people simply aren't a match (as was the case with Eric, who is now my business partner). Maybe you made mistakes, maybe you wish you could have done something different, but chances are this isn't the reason the relationship ended. (Unless you did something like cheat, in which case, it probably was something you did!)

It isn't because you weren't enough. I know this is how it might feel, but that is a destructive belief, and also a false one. Everyone has different things they want and need in a partner. There might be some things about you that one guy doesn't want, and those qualities may end up being what the right guy loves more than anything about you.

2. Feel Your Feelings

This can be the hard part, but it has to be done. Whatever it is you're feeling, feel it. Don't bury it, don't hide from it, don't ignore it. Feel the awful, brutal feelings. Mourn the loss, because a breakup is a loss. It's the loss of potential, the loss of what could have been.

In the beginning I'm sure you had grand visions of where this would go; that's because the beginning is always a euphoric time. But things didn't pan out the way you had hoped and you need to accept that.

Sometimes it can almost feel like a death when someone who was once so much a part of your life is now no longer in it, and that is very sad, even if you realize that this wasn't the right relationship for you. Give yourself time to grieve and be kind and gentle to yourself. Don't get mad at yourself for feeling what you're feeling; accept it as a part of the process. But don't let this drag on for too long. Life must go on and you'll never move forward if you keep mourning this loss. I would say give yourself a week, max, to let it all out, and then try to pick up the pieces.

3. Write Him A Letter You Don't Send

This can be a part of the grieving process, and while it may sound pointless, it is incredibly therapeutic and can assist in helping your feelings process.

After a breakup, your emotions will probably start spiraling all over the place. Rage, sadness, longing, anger, nostalgia, emptiness – you could feel it all in the span of just 30 minutes.

No matter what state you're in, write a letter with all the things you want to say to him, whether you're feeling fury and want to let him have it, or you're feeling nostalgic and want to reflect upon the happier times.

Whenever you feel an urge to reach out to him, or to speak to him, or even if you start thinking about things you wish you had said, just write it out in a letter. (I still have a bunch of mine and it's so wild looking at them all these years later!)

4. Surround Yourself With Love

The loss of someone who you shared a relationship with will inevitably leave a void that can make you feel empty and more alone than ever before. The best way to combat this feeling is to fill the hole with more love, either from family or friends. Don't isolate yourself from the world, get out there and rebuild some of those relationships that may have been neglected due to your relationship. Spend as much time as you can around people who truly love you and care about your happiness and wellbeing.

You should also immerse yourself in some self-love. Do some things just for you. Get a massage, a facial, buy a pair of amazing shoes. Give yourself a self-indulgent treat for no other reason than you love yourself and want to treat yourself kindly.

5. Do A Self-Check

Everything that happens in life, especially when it comes to breakups, has the potential to tear us down or take us to a higher place. As brutal as breakups are, they are a great time to do some reflection and inner work. Rather than stewing in feelings of hurt and pain, try to find a way to come out of this better than you were before. Here are a few good questions to ask yourself:

- What did I learn from this relationship that I can use in my next relationship?
- What did I do in this relationship that I won't ever do again in another relationship?
- What qualities do I truly need in a partner? (Think of qualities your ex had that you appreciated, as well as areas where he was lacking that you realized you need.)
- Why did I stay even though the relationship wasn't working?
- What did I learn about myself through my time with him?

6. Get Excited About Your Next Relationship

Once you have felt your feelings, found ways to love yourself, and learned the lessons that will help you be an even better person, get excited to use these newly acquired tools to have an even better relationship with a man who is even more suited for you.

I know how daunting it can feel to dive back into the dating pool, but don't focus on the annoying sides of dating, think of the exciting parts. Think about how thrilling a new relationship can be...that first date, the first kiss, the

THE ART OF LETTING GO

excitement that comes with the unlimited potential that lies ahead. Think about how amazing it will be to start clean with someone new – a blank slate, a new beginning. Think about what it will be like to be with a man who truly gets you, who appreciates you for the sum of all your parts, who cherishes you and would do anything to make you happy.

He exists; he's out there. You'll just have to have faith on that one because until he shows up, it can feel like you'll never find it, and then when you do, you'll wonder how you ever could have been worried about not finding it because what you have is just so right and it's so clear.

Finding the right guy entails two things. First, you must make yourself a vessel to receive love. You will never recognize the right guy when he comes along if you're still stuck on thoughts of the wrong guys. And you have to get over whatever issues are holding you back from receiving love. The next stage is to put yourself out there. Go out and date, get on the dating sites, download the dating apps. Most people think that this is the most important step, but it's not; this comes secondary to making yourself a vessel.

Trust me, I know how hard it is. I know how lonely it can feel. Heartbreak can be an isolating experience; it feels like this pain is yours and yours alone. Remember that you will get through it, just as many before you have.

You will heal, you will feel again, and you will find love, the right kind of love that will make you wonder how you ever mistook the wrong kind for the real thing.

While it can feel like fate has dealt you a brutal hand and life just isn't fair, try not to panic in the middle of the sentence because you truly have no idea how your story will unfold. Take my story as exhibit A, I never ever in my wildest dreams could have predicted I would marry the first guy who ever broke my heart and become business partners with an ex who hurt me so bad I felt like I had been gutted, but such is the story of my life!

Just because a relationship didn't work out doesn't mean it was a waste of time or it wasn't meant to be. Some people are meant to be in your life, you just won't and can't immediately know if they are meant to be in your life forever, or for a short period of time to teach you some sort of life lesson.

Rather than looking back on your former relationships with pain and regret, try to be grateful that you had the experience and recognize that it gave you something you needed, you might realize what it is now or maybe you'll see it later in life.

And above all, remember that you will get through this and you will be OK.

5

To The Lovers We Never Fully Let Go Of

Heidi Priebe

You know the ones.

They are the boys who catch your eye in hazy dive bars as the clock winds down to close, the girls whose laughter asks a question that your body wants to answer.

They are the ones who drive you accidentally mad. The ones who promise you absolutely nothing but deliver something you were never expecting; something exhilarating and tantalizing and oddly, unexpectedly comforting. Something you didn't think you'd get to hold onto but you suddenly don't want to let go.

You know the ones.

They fade in and out as the years go on – a stray text message there, vague plans to meet back up there. They are the people who exist on your periphery – always a city or a plane ride or a time zone or a life stage away. They are the people you keep track of from a distance, scrolling through news feeds and checking in on at 2am when a disappointing night winds to a close.

They are your maybe people, your someday people, your

'*what-if-in-a-different-world*' people, who offer the possibility you're lacking in this one.

And maybe we all need those lovers.

Maybe there's a quiet, unspoken part of us that craves that possibility more than its realization. Maybe we thrive on those maybes and those somedays more than we care to admit. Maybe we need to leave some doors open and some chapters unwritten. Maybe it's those maybes that keep us alive.

Because the truth about the lovers we cannot let go of is that maybe we don't want to ever realize each other's potential. Maybe we all like having someone to fantasize absentmindedly about, to send an open-ended text to every now and then, to catch up with over a leisurely bottle of wine every two to three years, when the geography and timing is right. Maybe all these people make up parts of ourselves that we don't want to ever fully realize, but want to keep alive.

We want to be the person who could still fall in love with the boy from three cities over, with the off-kilter laugh and the mind that spins and whirrs. We want to hold onto those drawn-out conversations with the girl who flips our world upside down with the patience in her spirit and her careful, measured thoughts. We need to keep all of these versions of ourselves and of each other alive, to remember that we're never at a loss for them.

That no matter how far we run or stray or falter, a different version of ourselves lives on inside of every person we have ever fallen half in love with. And we like having those versions to run back to. We like to keep them alive inside each other, in case we ever need to return to them.

In the strangest, most inexplicable way, we need those lovers that we never fully let go of.

Because each one of them represents a whole entire world within ourselves.

A world we aren't ready to let die. We aren't ready to abandon. We aren't willing to let go of completely.

At least, not yet.

Not yet.

6

It's Never Too Late To Start Over

Marisa Donnelly

It's never too late to start over. To hit the pause button. Breathe. Then begin again.

You don't need to lose yourself in the shuffle, get caught up in your mistakes and your fears and your anxieties. You don't have to hold onto your anger or your sadness and carry it with you in a little jar. You are more than a little jar, waiting to be filled by unsatisfying things—material things, superficial love, addictions and vices and so many other negatives that leave you feeling emptier than before. You are more than that little jar you feel defines the person you are, so much so that you try to fit yourself in its glass walls, try to keep contained within the edges and not overflow.

Life is imperfect. It's beautiful and complicated and burdensome and messy. And you are a part of it, a part that grows and changes and laughs and loves and gets broken and comes back together. But there will never be a time when you can't just step back and start all over.

There is no rewind, but you can always restart, let go. Let go of the toxic friends, of the urge to gossip, of the anxieties over what he said and she said, of the worry you feel over a future you cannot control. Let go. It's never too late to put down that jar of you're carrying and pull yourself out of it. Grab your legs and arms and brain and heart and soul and reconstruct them back into the self you're supposed to be. Reshape. Remold. Reconnect. And begin again.

You are not supposed to be this static person, this person you've always been and always will be. The world is continually shifting, and you are continually moving within it, in whatever direction you want. If you don't like that direction, turn. Don't turn back. Don't turn around. Just turn. Right. Left. Diagonal. Cut across the grass. Take a back road.

It's never too late to spin things around for the better. To leave what's been broken and acknowledge that you can't put it back together exactly how it was. To smile at the things you cannot replace, cannot fix, cannot make perfect. Nothing is perfect. You are not perfect. So don't drag around that little jar, the transparent jar of your imperfections for the world to see, for you to see as a constant reminder of the ways you've failed. Forget the jar. Forget how you've always been defined by it and define yourself by something new. Throw it down. Shatter it. Watch it fall and break and crush into a thousand tiny pieces and celebrate that change hurts, and that growth sucks. But now you are free falling, and it is terrifying, but terribly freeing.

Then start over. Begin again. All at once, or piece by piece. Start with the little things. Then be patient as you begin again, becoming new, becoming yourself.

7

You Were Never Enough For Me

Becca Martin

I was falling for the way you would show up and surprise me at my house. I was falling for the way you'd do sweet things without realizing how much they meant to me. I was falling for the way you kept your phone alarm set for me to wake up for work, even on mornings I wasn't there because you knew I'd need it another day. I was falling for the way you looked at me when we laid next to each other. I was falling for every piece of you from your goofy laugh to your rough hands.

I started falling the moment you sat down next to me at the bar and asked for my number after we talked for a while. Then a few short months after I stopped letting myself fall for you. I knew that had to be the end of it, and I presume you did too by the way things fell apart so gently and completely. It seemed we walked away from each other like it was nothing at all. The months I spent sleeping by your side and all the moments we shared together all just faded away ever so smoothly.

I can't recall what must have triggered that feeling; maybe it was because the last night we spent together you didn't hold me in your arms. Or maybe it was even because you didn't wrap your arms around me in the morning like you usually would. Whatever it was it was enough to make us realize it was over without saying a word. You drove me home and kissed me goodbye as I climbed out of your truck and watched you drive away, for the last time.

Just like that, without a word, we knew it was over.

Maybe it was because after all the time we spent together, I didn't feel the connection I read about having. I didn't feel sparks fly, even though I felt nerves when I saw you or turned down the dirt road leading to your driveway. I felt the warm happy feeling inside when you would say things that let me know you cared about me, but it still wasn't enough. I wasn't able to let you all the way in, maybe not even half way in.

I think it hit me then. I liked you and I wanted to like you with all my heart because it was easy and it was fun. But I couldn't. I don't think I'm ready to make the sacrifice to be in a relationship just yet and maybe he wasn't either because whatever happened that night, or maybe that morning, we both felt the end was here and we both seemed okay with it. It hurt a little, I felt a little sting of pain when I walked through my front door that morning, but I was comforted by the fact that I could just be alone, and not worry about someone else.

Life is the longest thing we'll ever do, but it also goes by quick. I do believe you should love the wrong person and experience heartbreak because it makes you stronger and smarter the next time around. But don't waste too much time loving someone who doesn't make you feel whole, don't spend time with someone who makes you wish you'd rather be single.

I was falling for the way you kissed me. I was falling for the way you made me laugh. I was falling for the way you found joy in the simplest things. I was falling for all the times you went out of your way to come see me. I was falling for the comfort I felt in turning to you about certain parts of my life.

But it still wasn't enough.

8

This Is Me Letting You Go

Heidi Priebe

This is me accepting that you're leaving. It's my acknowledgment that there's no further argument to make, no angle left to take, no plea or bargain I could wager that could get you to change your mind and stay. This is my subtle resignation to our downfall. This is the crack running between our two hearts that turned into a valley and engulfed us. It's my acceptance of all I couldn't bridge.

This is me knowing that we don't get a do-over – not on the last night I spent asleep beside you or the last time I told you I loved you or the first moment I felt us start to drift apart. I know we don't always get second chances. I know I do not get to go back in time and kiss you slower, love you stronger, linger five extra minutes in bed every morning that I woke up beside you. This is me knowing that I can't rewind history and ask you what was wrong each evening that you came home with a puzzle in your eyes but no answer on your lips. This is me knowing we don't get to go back.

This is my acceptance that I'm going to miss you. That there are going to be nights where I curl up in bed with a novel and a warm mug of tea and your absence on the left side of the bed is a chasm that swells and envelopes me. That for a long time I am going to see you everywhere – in second floor windows, in the faces of strangers, in the photos and memories that tear on my heartstrings for months after you're gone. This is the realization that missing you is going to become a second heartbeat in my body, strong and thrumming inside of every place where you lingered and then left. These are my weakened vital signs, beating out of sync with yours for a while.

This is my knowing life goes on. Knowing that someday I will not think of love as a feeling that's exclusive to you and I, as crazy as that seems to me right now. That eventually I'll meet someone new – someone who loves the foods you hate and laughs at things you don't find funny and appreciates the parts of me that you once left undiscovered. That some days, in the early morning hours, I'm going to wake up beside them and forget – just for an instant – that it is not your body tangled in mine. This is me knowing that those moments will defeat me – that I'm going to need to practice standing at the edge of your abyss without falling in completely. This is my hoping the discrepancy shrivels with time.

This is my conceptualization: That someday I'm going to have a wedding and that you will not be there. That the ring that gets slipped on my finger will be picked out by somebody else and that the people sitting in the front row with eyes brimming and hearts bursting will not be your family members. This is my acceptance of the finite absurdity of knowing that I'm someday going to promise my life to someone who is not you and that I may even be happy to do so. That one day I'll see changes and beginnings in a way I never saw them with you.

This is me knowing that we're going to grow old. That your life is going to be huge and important and chockfull of love but that it's all going to transpire without me. That I am not going to be there to toast to your 50th birthday or cheers to your timely promotion or crawl in beside you on the nights when the world's weight is too heavy to bear. That your losses and gains will not be lined up with mine. That someday when you hold your first-born child in your arms, it's not going to be me who placed her there.

This is me knowing that I have to let you go. That no matter how much I love you or how hard we work at this or how badly we both want each other to be happy, we are never going to be the right partners for each other. This is my acceptance that the best things are never straightforward and that I want you to take whatever crooked, twisted path you need to take if it will lead you towards your dreams. This is me knowing that I have to do what's right. That sometimes the best thing you can do for someone you love is to let them go – to do more, feel more, be more than the person they ever could ever have become by your side.

So this is me unclasping my fingers.

This is my parting, my reluctance, my heartache and my final gift to you.

This is me letting you go.

9

You Are Not For Everyone

Bianca Sparacino

You are not for everyone. There are poems within you that people will not be able to handle, storms surging through your bones that young men and women will never be able to weather.

See, you have a love inside of you that will ooze from your very veins like honey on a hot day and you will never be able to stop it. You're going to fall deeply in love with the wrong world – the kind of world young girls dream of, the kind of world where people say how they feel and love whom they love. You will forever be attached to the deep parts of those you tangle yourself within, though they will never get their hands dirty long enough to uncover the treasure that hums within your dancing pulse.

You are going to be misunderstood in the way you care, for you will love people not for what is obvious within them, but for what is hidden beneath their masks. You are not going to revel in their freckles, you will not compliment the hues within their eyes. You are going to live for the way they breathe in the cold December air, watching as their chest rises and falls like your very heartbeat. You are going to live for the way their pupils dilate when they talk about something they are truly passionate about, when their cheeks flush from a compliment or the unexpected brush of your foot against their leg.

No, you are not for everyone. You are never going to be able to stop yourself from screaming your love from rooftops, you will never be able to play it cool. You are the kind of person who will worry about the strangers you see in grocery stores, the kind of person who will stay up at night wondering about your fifth grade crush, hoping that the sun is setting beautifully wherever they rest their head.

For that, I hope you protect yourself.

I hope that you do not let the world condemn you for being too loud, too expressive, too soft; that you do not let it convince you to be perfect instead of real. I truly hope that you celebrate the fact that you are not for everyone, that you are not impressing the kinds of people who were built on the foundations of a sad world. If there is anything you do, please, let yourself rejoice in the fact that you do not fit in, that you think differently, because there is a chaos that laughs inside of you and it is going to change lives. It is going to make even the cynics believe again. It is going to grow love from thorn and glass.

10

You Have To Let Go Of The Things That Aren't Meant For You

Kovie Biakolo

Walt Whitman wrote, "Re-examine all that you have been told, and dismiss what insults your soul." Unfortunately for us, Whitman never left detailed instructions on exactly how to do this. And how do we really know the difference between the things that insult the soul, and the things that though difficult to practice, keep the soul firm, strong, and honest? It seems rather easy to dismiss anything that we find difficult to live by, or go through, under the guise that, "it is not meant for you." But difficulties, uncomfortable situations, and the struggles we face, do more than give us grief and great stories – they temper the soul. And they make the spirit both humble and resilient.

Yet if you observe clearly – both others and yourself – you will find that people hold on tightly to things, especially onto beliefs that certain things are meant for them. And this manifests itself in different ways. From destructive relationships, to an inflexibility in changing one's career path or vocation, to the unwillingness to constantly reflect on one's fundamental values, much less change them. We hold on tightly to things because it is very easy to form habits. And our habits – whether they are our thoughts, words, or actions – are not easy to break.

Think of something that you really wanted, that you thought was meant for you. Maybe it's even something that you had, but lost; something you eventually ended up without. It hurt, didn't it? And maybe it hurt so badly that you just couldn't quite let it go. And holding on to it, in its own strange way, felt like you still had it. But this sensation, this obsession that we have for the things that we hold onto tightly – our grip seemingly unbreakable – rarely, if ever, keeps us from loss. We lose things all the time – "the Lord giveth and the Lord taketh away," as Job warned us in the Old Testament.

One way to be kinder to people, I think, is to remember that we have all lost something, and many have lost a great deal. Sometimes the loss is so difficult to bare, that even the illusion that whatever we wanted is still with us, is better than nothing at all. And then we go through life with a tight grip on everything that has already escaped us. The fear of letting things that we oftentimes think define us, or keep us whole, supersedes the courage that we are capable of, of choosing the unknown, and letting the familiar leave us.

But here's what I know, and it's probably one of the few things I actually really know: Tighter grips on the things that aren't meant for us, close us to life. And you have to be open to life. If you're not open, you're going to hold onto things that will bring you *unnecessary* pain and suffering. If you are open, life still brings you pain, but it will be the kind of pain that is *necessary* to get you where you are destined to be. Even if this destiny might be drastically different from the path you're on right now. And maybe this is where Whitman's counsel comes in – knowing the difference between the necessity of our suffering, allows us to keep what is meaningful, and to throw away the unnecessary pains; to throw away what insults the soul.

If you don't trust anything or anyone in life, trust that the things you leave behind allow you to make room for the unexpected. Because with enough faith, courage, hope, and love; and the awareness of every blessing we've been given, and feeling gratitude for every gift we've been granted, the unexpected paths we end up taking, often end up feeling like the place we are exactly meant to be.

In the end, our paths are rarely straight and narrow, and they were never meant to be anyway. And if all we do in each one is learn a lesson, or meet a friend, or know ourselves better, or do something kind for someone, we have done much. But first, first we must have the courage to let go of the things that are not meant for us.

11

How To Let Go Of Grief

Lauren Jarvis-Gibson

You can't ever forget a first love, but you can let go of them eventually. You can't ever forget a loved one who passed away, but you can eventually continue on with your life and heal. I wish there could be a magical spell to stop all the pain and memories, but that would be too easy wouldn't it?

I know the grief that is felt after loss. It covers you like a blanket and threatens to choke you with its enormous weight. It follows you around and tries to trip you as soon as you get back on your feet. It haunts you in your sleep and you can't even run away from it in your dreams.

But, what I have come to find is that grief isn't your enemy. Your rejection of grief is. Too many times, we try to hide from our deep emotions and try to make a shield to protect ourselves from them. But too many times, this is the wrong thing to do. We are only hurting ourselves more by continuing to ignore our hurt.

The first and final step to let go of someone is to grab onto grief's hand and let it take you on a ride. Just be prepared, it is going to hurt like hell. You will cry. You will scream. You will hurt and you will ache. But it only will go up from here. It will only get better from this starting point.

You will have days where the nostalgia returns and you can't even breathe because you miss them so much. You will have days where you just want to sit in bed and cry staring at the letters they wrote to you. But, you will also have days where you wake up clear headed and nothing reminds you of them. You will have days where you hear their name, and you don't even flinch.

The more you realize that it's okay to feel what you are feeling, the more you heal. The more you walk beside grief instead of running from it, the more you heal. So, instead of ignoring grief, shake its hand and greet your sadness with open arms. Don't expect to be healed in a week. Don't expect to be cured in a month. Just expect gaining love and respect for yourself as you step into this journey without looking back.

12

Read This If You Don't Understand Why Someone Doesn't Like You

Ellen Nguyen

When someone doesn't want you, in the beginning, it will be hard. Sometimes, very hard. You will think there is something wrong with you, something so undesirable and unlovable that definitely needs to be fixed and changed. You will try to recall every tiny detail of what happened, examining like it's a case file and you're the lead detective just so you could pinpoint a reason why life didn't go the way you wanted. But there is never a satisfying answer because even if it was the answer given by that person — most likely one to gently let you down, your bruised ego would refuse to believe it anyway.

That's how endless questions won't stop circling in your head and soon you will start to believe you are not good enough, or worse, happiness isn't what you deserve. Once self-doubt and cruel thoughts start creeping in, you will be forced to face all your insecurities and be reminded of all the times you were left behind and not chosen. Even the wounds that you were certain had been healed seem to be torn apart and cut wide open again. You will feel small and insignificant but all at the same time unbearably heavy.

Luckily, over time, it will get better. You might never fully forget but your pain will be relieved and you will eventually stop thinking about them every waking second. You will come to terms with the fact that they are not here with you and life goes on whether you want it to or not. But unfortunately, it doesn't mean you will stop questioning and hating yourself for all that happened, for everything that could have been. It's like you were shot but the bullet has never been removed so it keeps aching from the inside.

As memories take you right back to where you were, you will wish for the millionth time that you could be someone else — someone prettier, smarter, cooler. Then perhaps you wouldn't have to hear the dreadful "but" after "I think you are a very great person." Perhaps things would have turned out differently. Perhaps you would have known what it is like to be on their mind, to be the receiver of every "I miss you" that is meant every single word, and for once, to be the one that is wanted instead of getting so close to the desire of your heart but never being able to have it.

Be prepared because the flood of sentiments will not hit you just once. It will happen many, many times and each time it will hurt like the first as if you haven't moved on at all. Maybe you really haven't, especially if after all this time you still don't understand why it cannot be you, beating yourself up over the ending you somehow messed up. You will ask yourself all over again what it is that you're lacking and what it is that you need to have to be deserving of their love. You will see flaws and imperfections in every reflection of yourself and never truly feel complete.

But please listen to me. This is important. What you fail to see and need to know now to set your heart free is that you have been asking all the wrong questions and to the questions you can't stop asking, the answers have always been right in front of your eyes: That person doesn't want to be with you. They are not here with you. They have made a conscious choice for their own sake to be where they are now. It happens. Simple as that. You don't need to have the reasons why.

And seriously, what's good in knowing?

The truth is, when someone doesn't want you, no reason matters. No amount of fixing could change that and actually, there isn't anything that needs to be fixed because nothing was wrong or missing in the first place. You have always been wholly you, before or after them, including all the flaws and imperfections that make you unique. So if you ever feel the need to redeem or validate yourself after being rejected, please don't because no one can take anything away from you by not wanting you and you aren't born to prove yourself to anyone.

It might be hard to fathom all this when you have invested so much energy and time into this said person and are clouded by the pain from their rejection but if you put things into perspective, if you look back at all the times you say no to the people who want you but for some reason are just not quite right, you will be able to make sense of your own situation and stop blaming yourself so much. You will find it easier to accept that not everyone chooses you and it's okay because you respect and love yourself enough to let go of the past and keep going to those who want you the same way and love you for all what you are.

With all that being said, if you don't feel whole by yourself, if you believe you need to be filled, if you haven't quite known who you are and learned to love yourself yet, having someone's interest is never the solution. It's not going to magically make all that happen. In fact, nothing could, except you. You have the power to take yourself to a place of peace and acceptance. You have the choice to be kinder to yourself each day. You are capable of making decisions that add positivity to your life and shape you into a better person.

When someone doesn't want you, one day you will be thankful for their honesty and decision because they have let you go on to find yourself and the happiness you deserve. Such happiness will not only help you realize how strong and brave you have been but it also shows you exactly why things didn't work out with anyone before.

13

When The One You Could Love Forever Slips Away

Beau Taplin

To my sweetheart, my teacher, and kindred spirit.

What a senseless fool I have been and how ashamed I am for allowing you to slip away, for letting my past stand in the way of something so extraordinary, present and sincere. But this isn't a time for excuses or apologies. Heaven knows you have heard enough these last few weeks and I am now out of ways to express the enormous regret I feel and acknowledge that admitting to, or apologizing for my actions and mistakes does not make amends for them. Neither would I have you believe that this is a desperate plea to win back your affections. I am tired and ashamed of dampening your days with my desperate pressing and I never intend to do so again. Rather, I am writing you because anything else would be insincere. I am writing you because I adore you and nothing can be done about it. I am writing you because there are things that must be said and I can think of nothing else but you.

I remember, with every available minute, how soft and

simple the days were with you. How each one fell gently into the arms of the next and instead of feeling trapped or anxious thinking ahead to the future, I wished, for the very first time in my life, that time would begin to slow down. That things would stay sweet and gentle, as they were, and that I would never taint or make a mess of all that was free and joyful in us.

You have always been someone I have respected enormously. Your mind is extraordinary, and the way you perceive the world around you with such enthusiasm and wonder moves me to do the same. I am so proud of all that you do, and all that you are. And the pleasure of seeing you apply yourself and achieve such spectacular heights motivates the people around you to push and fight harder for their own wishes and dreams.

There is never a dull moment with you. You move me to be more present and in tune with the world around me, and have a manner of making even the most mundane thing utterly magic and unforgettable. Every day with you has been a pleasure and a gift, and my god, you have made me happy and whole. You captivate me with your passions and send me positively mad with want and need. I want to roll around with you on the floor. See you dance and turn in the low light. Push my lips to that devilish grin again. Feel my hands on your hands and everywhere else. You make me wild and naive and a single kiss from you is enough to send me to ecstasy. You have this extraordinary energy about you that consumes and calms me all at once, and the way you dismantle my defenses and challenge me at every turn helps me to become a stronger and more passionate person. I feel capable of anything around you—you bring out my best self.

I love you, precious. It has been a privilege to love you. It is a privilege to love you. And though every day without you is agony and things between us have become messy and painful, there is a relief in knowing, at last, with absolute certainty, precisely what it is I want. I would like you to know that not a single day will go by where I would not give the world, and my very best, to make amends, to shelter and serve you, and know the immeasurable privilege of having your heart and trust with me once more. I adore you. You have been a true light in my life. And if nothing else, let these words speak to the profound and wonderful influence you have on the lives you touch. You certainly did on mine.

14

If They Leave You, You Must Let Them Go

Ari Eastman

"If he leaves, you have to let him go." My mother sits at the kitchen table, offering up this simple sentence. I want to tell her it isn't that easy and I don't understand why. She gently pushes a plate of food towards me, but I'm not hungry. Her eyes are green, just like mine. I can see the worry. I want to tell her I'm okay.

But in that moment, I'm not.

"But why would he say those things? I don't understand. Nothing makes sense." I stare at my hands because I'm afraid to look straight at my mom. We have faced unimaginable demons together, taking turns at the helm. We have steered ships straight through storms, together. We are Athenas, strong and resilient. We are warriors, and I know this. But a boy has left me and I can't stop crying. I want to ask her how I can stand so tall against boulders, but he throws a pebble and I come apart.

"Not everything makes sense. And sometimes, trying will drive you insane," she offers.

I have learned people can say the opposite of what they

mean. Or maybe even worse? They can mean it. They can say things with full honesty. They want you and love you. Everything is real and authentic. But it changes. Our feelings, our hopes, our wants, can change with such quickness, it leaves you spinning in the driveway. I watch him walk out of the apartment with a new decision. He will be with her now. He wants her now.

But I still ask myself: Why? Why do I feel so much and he suddenly has changed his mind?

———————

If they leave, you have to let them go. Because otherwise? You will sit waiting in the driveway. Your stomach will land inside your mouth with every headlight you see. You will become convinced each car is theirs. That this next one, that will be it. They will come back. That it was all a dream, or a nightmare. So you sit. And you wait. The sun sets and comes back up, and you're still waiting.

But my darlings, if you wait too long, the sun will keep setting and rising and you will have not moved. I'm not saying they won't ever come back. Maybe they do. Maybe they don't. Hell, I'm no clairvoyant. I do not know your situation or your outcome. But if they have left, you have to let them go. You have no other choice. Because they made this decision. They could have stayed.

And they didn't.

I'm sorry. I want to hug you right now because that's harsh and it hurts. But they made a deliberate choice of their own free will. I don't know why. Maybe you don't either. But it happened. And now is the time for you.

It is your time. Look at that sun setting, isn't it beautiful? Okay, that's cheeseball and I'm sorry, but SERIOUSLY. Look at that damn sun! The sun is a giant star 92,960,000 miles from Earth and here you are, looking at it. It is the most important source of life for our planet and here you are, looking at it. That is something to take in. We are all so sure our problems, especially of the romantic nature, are the end of universes, but the sun keeps burning.

So you need to keep burning. You are a star on Earth, and again, I'm sorry if I'm being melodramatic, but hey — someone's got to remind you. Someone left you and now you're wondering if you are just ash. Are you the aftermath of a star exploding? No. You are a star reaching new heights. You are learning to be okay with your place in the sky. Shooting stars are the cowards, running away. You, my love, you are here. You did not run.

If they leave, kiss them goodbye and mean it. Maybe you were too bright and beautiful for them. Let them leave. Move forward with who you are meant to be, separate of them. You may crumble and wonder if it's worth it.

You are.

———————

"How can I let him go?" I ask my mom once more, hoping this time it will be an answer that automatically clicks.

"You just do. Maybe slowly, maybe it takes time. But eventually, *you do*."

15

The Truth About Changing Them

Kim Quindlen

You won't. Because you can't.

Whether you know it now, or you're still in the process of learning this truth, at some point you will understand that the only person you can control in your life is yourself. Other people can be manipulated, bullied, guilted, pleaded with. But the only way they are going to truly change is of their own accord, from the inside out.

But it feels better to just hope for change anyway, to hope that they start behaving differently so that you can fix (what's left of) your relationship. So that you don't have to start over, completely lost, after who knows how many months, or years. When you've given so much of yourself to a relationship and to another person, it seems so much easier to stay, and hope that eventually they'll magically be different, than it is to let go and move on.

Sometimes, the change really is necessary: they're abusive, or unfaithful, or unbelievably selfish, or even just completely apathetic to the relationship. Sometimes, the change is just something you need from a relationship that they seem to be lacking: you wish they were more lighthearted, you wish they cared more about family, you wish they liked the same things you did.

But whether the desire for change is out of righteousness or plain old preference is irrelevant, because it's not something you will ever have the power to bring about. You can beg, hope, ask, plead, blackmail, tempt, motivate, guilt. But you will never be able to change their essence, unless they want to change.

That's one of the hardest parts about relationships. Understanding the difference between being flexible and willing to compromise, versus standing your ground when you know you deserve better. The difference between having high standards and finding a person who truly loves you, versus having a demanding, ridiculous list of expectations, none of which you are willing to bend on and all of which are impossible to uphold at the same time.

But it's also one of the keys to being happy in your love life. Being able to understand when to stay, and when to walk away. When you're being shallow and high-maintenance, and when you're just being firm about the treatment you know you deserve.

You can't force someone to love you, to treat you a certain way. To be honest, faithful, supportive, and kind. But you can love yourself enough to acknowledge when you're being treated wrongly and when you deserve better.

It's not about changing them. It never has been. If you're doing research and brainstorming ways that you can 'fix' them, you're fighting a losing battle. The only direction you should be turning is inward. Listen to yourself, listen to your gut. If they're mistreating you in some way, you'll know. If you're just being overly demanding, you'll know (if you really, honestly listen to yourself). You do not have the power to change them. What you do have is the power to decide whether or not you're going to stay.

16

Read This If You Can't Forget Someone Who Has Already Forgotten You

Rania Naim

There are two main reasons why we struggle to forget someone: 1) We truly believe they are the one for us. 2) We fear that we will not find anyone better. However, we should all remember two things: 1) If someone *is* the right person for us, they will come back into our lives no matter how far away they drift. 2) You will always be able to find someone better—or, rather, someone just as good who won't forget you.

Feeling forgotten or neglected by someone you care deeply about can be one of the most soul-crushing & excruciating feelings in the world. Instead of forcing yourself to try, in vain, to forget that person, I want you to free yourself to remember them.

Remember them when you are alone at night crying, remember the pain they put you through, remember when you almost lost your breath because of the tears you shed over them, and remember how you had to hide your eyes behind your sunglasses so no one could see them, or see *you*.

Remember them on your birthday, remember how they are actively choosing not to celebrate another year with you, **remember that they are happier celebrating somewhere else, maybe with someone else**. Remember that they want to grow old without you.

Remember them when you are lonely, remember how they once promised not to leave you, remember how they could have turned your loneliness around but they left you staring at all four walls as they found someone else to ease their lonely nights.

Remember them when you attend an engagement party or a wedding, remember that instead of being your plus one, they left you minus one. Remember that they convinced you that you were heading in that direction but suddenly decided to make a U-turn and drove away on their own.

Remember them when your family asks about your relationship status, remember how you could have easily avoided that question had they been there to answer it. **Remember that they didn't want to give you an answer or even help you find it.**

Remember them when you are having a blast with your friends, remember that this is how they should've made you feel, but they decided to be strangers. They decided they'd rather treat you like a *stranger* not a friend.

Remember them when you are smiling because someone appreciates you, remember how they didn't, and remember how they slowly took that smile away from you. **Remember that they chose to make someone else smile instead.**

Remember them every time you want to forget them,

remember that they are not remembering you, and remember that they want you to forget them.

Remember them when you finally get over them, remember them when you see them and no longer recognize them.

17

You Broke My Heart, But I Am Forever Thankful

Marisa Donnelly

I wasn't supposed to fall in love with you. You were dangerous eyes and a quick temper. You were argumentative and stubborn and so wonderfully compassionate. I got lost in those eyes and felt safe in those arms.

We began as nothing. I told myself we were just having fun. That smiles were because we enjoyed each other's company. That kisses were playful. That we were happy, not falling.

I never meant to kiss so deeply. I never imagined that your arms around me would feel like home. And I don't know if you did either. Maybe it was a line we accidentally crossed, dancing in a bar just a little after midnight, the voices around us all melting away. Dancing, spinning, spinning. Or maybe it was when we explored each other's minds on a couch in your living room, confessing secrets we'd been too afraid to share. Opening slowly, learning to trust again.

I wasn't supposed to fall in love with you, but I did. Layer by layer. And I think you did, too. It happened exactly like the world says, slowly, then all at once. Suddenly we were sharing pillows and paychecks and dreams. Suddenly those three words, the 'I love yous' whispered at night, in the morning, as I dropped you off, when you picked me up, carried incredible weight.

But then we unfolded, as beautiful things often do. We were both at fault, maybe more than we wanted to admit. We fought hard. Me with words. You with those dangerous eyes, that quick temper. We cracked, shattered into tiny pieces that were too difficult to put back together, but a part of me still believed.

But then came the heartbreak. It was unexpected, yet a part of me knew it was inevitable. I had fallen. I was breakable. I wasn't supposed to be in love with you. I wasn't supposed to be hurt. But I was, just the same. And you had transformed into someone I no longer knew, someone I didn't think you were anymore, someone I never thought you could be. It broke me. It unraveled me into little threads of myself. Little fragments of my heart that I knew would take so long to mold back together.

But I forgave you.

In time. After tears. As I woke to the sun on a new day and saw the freedom, the lifted weight on my heart, in forgiving you. You were the boy with dangerous eyes, with arms that sheltered me. You were the boy whose home I discovered, whose heart I opened. The boy who had held my own heart in his hands. Together we had re-learned how to love, how to let someone in when you are still fragile, still scared. We had fallen in love. And because of this, I am forever thankful.

I am thankful for poolside drinks, for dog walks, for drives with the windows down. I am thankful for the swing you built me in the backyard, for the smell of your deodorant, for the picture frame in your room with the photos of us, laughing, smiling, dancing, spinning, spinning.

You broke my heart, but I am forever thankful. For the moments, the memories, the kisses, and the accidental falling that happens when you close your eyes, when you let it. For what I learned in losing you: what I deserve, the immensity of my strength, my capacity to love, to let go. For you. I hope you know that you are forgiven. But I still hope when you kiss her, you taste me. And maybe one day you'll forgive yourself.

18

The Truth About Why I Don't Contact You Anymore

Ellen Nguyen

I didn't contact you because I didn't want you to misinterpret my intention. In fact, I had no intention other than I thought of you and it would be genuinely great to hear from you. But I knew you would read between the lines, looking for a hidden meaning underneath my *hello*. You would expect from *What have you been up to*? more than just a lukewarm conversation. Something like an active interest, an invitation, a plan. And If I must be honest, I'm really not in a place to deliver any of those things in any shape or form. Nor could I take responsibility for the "I miss you" that I might slip out on the spur of the moment.

I might want to come to you again, yet for all the wrong reasons. Like last time when I texted you at 4 o' clock after a dead party and you told me I could come over, I would've totally thrown away all my rationale and found my way back into your arms and probably your bed if it hadn't been for some circumstantial inconvenience. The problem is, it isn't because I wanted to be with you. It's because it was 4 a.m and I was drunkenly desperate for a warm body to comfort mine. What's even worse is that you might just want the same thing and I would end up feeling as though I was a pathetic mess having no self-respect whatsoever.

So tell me. What if it happens again? How do I resist your interest, invitation and plan? How could I keep being stupid and making decisions that do me no good? Obviously, I can't and I won't. If it was a year ago, you would probably get a text back within 30 seconds of contacting me and my lips would be all over yours again. I would give no shit about the impracticality of us despite being very well aware I would be the one to get hurt in the end. But I'm 21 now and I don't want trouble any more. I'm no longer thrilled by the sign of danger and moments that give me instant gratification but would ultimately ruin me. I've been through enough to see our ending before we even begin again so please let me save us the hassles.

That being said, to be fair, it's not just about you. I don't contact you or anyone because really, right now, I need time for myself. It doesn't matter how great someone is — at this stage of life, I'm not ready for a "we" and I'm happy being on my own. There are so many things I would like to do for myself and my future and I wouldn't be able to give it my best if my time and energy were invested elsewhere. More importantly, I have no clue where I will be in a year or two. I don't want to get involved with someone and have one foot out the door while pretending I can be the chill girl doing casual stuff. I'm not chill and I don't want to be casual with the people I like. I want to be all in. I want to make promises when I'm capable of keeping and turning them into real actions. Realistically, now is not the time for that yet.

If there's no response from me, it doesn't mean my heart has been immune to human affection. Many times, I have thought and have deleted a text half-way through. Many times, I have waited if there was another message after my silence. Many times, I have wished that someone would try to break my walls and show my stubborn mind how wrong it could be. Because my door might be closed but it's not locked yet. After all, I'm still a woman and sometimes a woman wants to have a man by her side and her womanly desires fulfilled. But I guess, unfortunately, I can't have my cake and eat it too.

It's all right, though. I'm 21 now and if there's anything worthwhile I have learned, it must be about patience and self-control. I will wait and stay grounded for the life I aspire to lead and because I know the things I truly want are not readily available. It takes time. For now, I don't mind having my phone quiet.

19

Here's How To Stop Loving Them

Ari Eastman

When you decide to stop loving them, your body will convince you this is the wrong decision. Everything inside burns with promises, with ideas about the future, with a different you. The you before the shattering. Before the ending. Before you were faced with the strangling thought that now, you are not supposed to love them anymore. Now, you are supposed to move on from this feeling.

Open up a box with all the memories you're trying to forget. Scatter them across the entire room, taking your time to not miss a single moment. Sit with all of it. Wonder if you can still smell someone on a shirt you haven't worn in so many moons. Do not run to the bottle or cell phone, ready to send messages you'll regret when the melancholy isn't aching so loudly. Just sit there.

Remember how it felt when they kissed your clavicle, or how their laugh always reminded you of a stampede. Wildebeest herd be damned, you'd risk being trampled every time.

Think about the first time your heart told you this feeling

was different from before. It wasn't the love you'd heard of. This is the kind that bubbles up, an unwatched pot of water ready to explode. There is a power in it you cannot turn down.

Silently curse it. And then, verbally curse it. Look at all these ghosts of happier times and think how no one warned you of the leftover haunting. Saying goodbye doesn't mean everything ends.

Feel dirty, ashamed, like you should be better than this. Like you should know how to be okay. But you're not. So, yell. Yell to no one and everyone.

Store the box away. If it feels right, maybe you'll throw it out entirely. Just let it be out of sight right now.

Feel for your pulse. Marvel that every day, your heart beats about 100,000 times. It feels like you think of them 100,000 times. But your heart is still beating and pumping. Even though it feels broken, it's still going. And so are you.

Watch a movie or comedy special that forces laughter from your lips. One of those strong belly type laughs can send 20% more blood flowing, so giggle even when you aren't sure you can. Watch Aziz Ansari, or Amy Schumer, or John Mulaney, pick your favorite. Feel hearty bellows healing your body. Remember your heart is not broken. Broken things do not continue working. You are bruised. But you still *work*.

Call or reach out to someone who has always been there for you — a friend or family member. Tell them five different reasons they matter to you and how much you value your relationship with them. Sip on some nostalgia and joke about a story from your past together. Romantic love, while beautiful, is only *one* kind of love, and never enough to fully sustain a person. Take note of all the people you have in your life. All the love you have surrounding.

Go for a walk and make yourself a promise for the duration of your walk. *I will allow myself to feel whatever I feel.* And listen. With every step, check in with yourself. Are you sad? Are you angry? Do you feel utterly lost? Listen to all of it. Accept all of it. Decide this walk will be the time you finally let yourself off the hook. Decide this walk will be when you are allowed to grieve however you need.

Cry. Question. Break and look them up on social media. Want to cry more. Think of calling them. Of texting. Don't.

When you decide to stop loving them, you will do everything you can think of to make it come true. But maybe you aren't ready to stop. Maybe time, distance, or some other magic ingredient will do the trick. Or maybe, just maybe, it's okay to still love them. Perhaps your heart has enough room for some piece of love to stay forever. A preserved painting. An artifact of what you shared. An echo in the back of your chest. You will figure it out.

And if after all this, you still find yourself loving them, so what? We could all use more love, even if it's the type to be tucked away in a box.

20

What You Should Do When You Want To Run Back To Them

Kim Quindlen

You're alone and it sucks. The sadness and isolation that you feel is sickeningly heavy. You've replayed the breakup a thousand times. You've imagined a thousand different reconciliation scenarios. Everything else happening in your life seems disconnected from your mental processing; this is the only thing you can think about.

Your equilibrium is off. You don't know how to sort out anything you're currently feeling. You've been through so many emotional highs and lows in such a short amount of time that you can't really tell the difference between missing this person and simply missing love.

How do you know you're doing the right thing? How do you know you're not making a mistake?

The instinct will be to run back to them – to do it without thinking, to follow your impulse, to "listen to your heart." That's because we're conditioned to believe that that's love. We've seen it in movies, watched it on tv, heard it in a thousand love songs. But that's not really love. It's just a good storyline. The desperation, the race to win someone back, the dramatization of it all – that keeps us interested, watching, listening.

So we think that's how we're supposed to behave in real life, too. But real life doesn't happen in 105 minutes, with a set-up, problem, climax, and resolution. It doesn't happen in a tender, 3-minute song or a touching, 22-minute season finale.

As beautiful as they are to listen to, love stories don't involve the eloquent, well-articulated, Shonda-esque monologues that you see on *Grey's Anatomy*. Love stories and breakups do not unfold the way they do in a beautiful, well-lit Taylor Swift video. Rather, the processes you go through, and the pain you try to sort out, happen in boring, uneventful moments of life that are typically left out of a story.

You deal with your breakup, you feel the emotions, and you come to certain conclusions while you're cleaning out the fridge, or scrolling through Netflix in your pajamas, or sorting through junk mail. You probably don't look great. Your apartment is probably a mess. You'd rather be anywhere else than laying on your couch or sitting at your desk at work.

Maybe you actually are meant to be together. Maybe this breakup is something you both need to mature, to understand yourselves as individuals, to figure out that this is truly what you want. Or maybe you're not meant to be together. Maybe you're supposed to be alone for a while, or you're supposed to meet someone else, or you're supposed to focus on something other than love at this moment in your life.

But either way, you will never know if you run back to them right now. Right now is the time for you to live the beauty of a normal, painful, sometimes boring, three-dimensional life. You're not a character in a Thursday night television series, you're not a line in a song, you're not the star of the latest Nancy Myers film. You're a real person, which is so much better, even when it doesn't seem like it.

The pain you will go through in your life (right now, and in the future) is so much worse than something a character will experience in a five-minute character-building montage. But the joys, the highs, and the love that you will feel are so much better, too.

But it comes at a price, and this is the price. You cannot get over this breakup (or reach your reconciliation) by romanticizing your experience. You just have to go through it in all of its unappealing glory. You have to feel it. You have to let it wash over you when you're doing laundry. And eventually, with time, you will know what is right. You will know whether or not you should fight for this person, whether or not you're meant to go back to each other. You will know it in your gut. It's just going to take longer than a well-written 2-minute scene, set by a fountain in New York City on a bright, sunny day.

21

8 Reasons To Thank The People Who Hurt You Most In Life

Brianna Wiest

1. The people who were able to hurt you most were also the people who you were able to love the most.

We aren't profoundly affected by people who aren't already deeply within our hearts. For someone to have that much importance in your life is sacred, even when it goes askew. It's a gift to know someone who was able to truly affect you, even if at first, it didn't seem like it was for the best.

2. Difficult relationships often push you to change your behavior for the better.

In feeling helpless, you learn to take care of yourself. In feeling used, you recognize your worth. In being abused, you develop compassion. In feeling like you're stuck, you realize there is always a choice. In accepting what was done to you, you realize that nobody has control at the end of the day, but in surrendering the need for something we'll never have, we can find peace, which is what we were actually seeking in the first place.

3. What you learn and who you become is more important than how you temporarily feel.

That relationship may have seemed almost unbearable at the time, but the feeling is transitory. The wisdom and grace and knowledge that you carried with you afterwards isn't. It sets a foundation for the rest of your life. The ends far outweigh the means, and to be grateful for what you've been through is to completely acknowledge that.

4. You don't come across these people by accident, they were your teachers and catalysts.

In the words of C. Joybell C., we're all stars that think they're dying until we realize we're collapsing into supernovas – to become more beautiful than ever before. It often takes the contrast of pain to completely appreciate what we have, it often takes hate to incite self-recognition. Sometimes the way light enters us is, in fact, through the wound.

5. Even if it wasn't your fault, it is your problem, and you get to choose what you do in the aftermath.

You have every right to rage and rant and hate every iota of someone's being, but you also have the right to choose to be at peace. To thank them is to forgive them, and to forgive them is to choose to realize that the other side of resentment is wisdom. To find wisdom in pain is to realize that the people who become 'supernovas' are the ones who acknowledge their pain and then channel it into something better, not people who just acknowledge it and then leave it to stagnate and remain.

6. The people who have been through a lot are often the ones who are wiser and kinder and happier overall.

This is because they've been "through" it, not "past" it or "over" it. They've completely acknowledged their feelings and they've learned and they've grown. They develop compassion and self-awareness. They are more conscious of who they let into their lives. They take a more active role in creating their lives, in being grateful for what they have and in finding reason for what they don't.

7. It showed you what you do deserve.

Those relationships didn't actually hurt you, they showed you an unhealed part of yourself, a part that was preventing you from being truly loved. That's what happens when we finally get past hurtful experiences and terrible relationships: we realize we are worth more, and so we choose more. We realize how we blindly or naively said "yes" to someone or gave them our mind and heart space when we didn't have to. We realize our role in choosing what we want in our lives, and by experiencing what seems like the worst, we finally acknowledge that it feels so wrong because we deserve so much more.

8. Truly coming to peace with anything is being able to say: "Thank you for that experience."

To fully move on from anything, you must be able to recognize what purpose it served, and how it made you better. Until that moment, you'll only be ruminating in how it made things worse, which means you're not to the other side yet. To fully accept your life – the highs, lows, good, bad – is to be grateful for all of it, and to know that the "good" teaches you well, but the "bad" teaches you better.

22

20 Quotes To Read If You Can't Let Someone Go

Rania Naim

1. *Letting go doesn't mean that you don't care about someone anymore. It's just realizing that the only person you really have control over is yourself.*—Deborah Reber

2. *There ain't no way you can hold onto something that wants to go, you understand? You can only love what you got while you got it.*—Kate DiCamillo

3. *At some point you will realize that you have done too much for someone, that the only next possible step to do is to stop. Leave them alone. Walk away. It's not like you're giving up, and it's not like you shouldn't try. It's just that you have to draw the line of determination from desperation. What is truly yours will eventually be yours, and what is not, no matter how hard you try, will never be.*—Unknown

4. *If they weren't good for you in 2015, they won't be great for you in 2016. Let them go.*—Robert Tew

5. *Let go of the attachment, keep the lesson.*—L.J. Vanier

6. *Sometimes you have to forget what you feel and remember what you deserve.*—Unknown

7. *You didn't love her, you just didn't want to be alone. Or maybe, maybe she was good for your ego, or maybe she made you feel better about your miserable life, but you didn't love her, because you don't destroy the person that you love.*—Shonda Rhimes

8. *Some people believe holding on and hanging in there are signs of great strength. However, there are times when it takes much more strength to know when to let go and then do it.*—Ann Landers

9. *It doesn't matter if its a relationship, a lifestyle, or a job. If it doesn't make you happy, let it go.*—Unknown

10. *And sometimes good things fall apart so better things can fall together.*—Marilyn Monroe

11. *She's not going to let go until she sees for herself that there's nothing left to hold on to.*—Susane Colasanti

12. *The longer you're with the wrong person, you could be completely overlooking the chance to meet the right person.*—Taylor Swift

13. *Sometimes removing some people out of your life makes room for better people.*—Unknown

14. *Why don't you tell me that 'if the girl had been worth having*

she'd have waited for you'? No, sir, the girl really worth having won't wait for anybody.—F. Scott Fitzgerald

15. *Detach yourself just when you realize you are closer to a heart break.*—Unknown

16. *You can meet someone who's just right, but he might not be meant for you. You break up, you lose things, you never feel the same again. But maybe you should stop questioning why. Maybe you should just accept it and move on.*—Winna Efendi

17. *Life isn't about waiting for the storm to pass, it's about learning to dance in the rain.*—Vivian Greene

18. *Holding on is believing that there's only a past; letting go is knowing that there's a future.*—Daphne Rose Kingma

19. *Someday, someone will walk into your life and make you realize why it never worked out with anyone else.*—Unknown

20. *What's meant to be will always find a way.*—Trisha Yearwood

Made in the USA
Las Vegas, NV
11 December 2023

82452659R00059